PROJECT

Puppy

Jakki Wood

W
FRANKLIN WATTS
NEW YORK • LONDON • SYDNEY

If you choose me to be your puppy –

I'll be your best friend.

I can't wait to explore my new home, especially my bed. I'm still a baby so I'll need lots of naps.

At first, I'll miss cuddling up to my brothers and sisters in the night.
A warm hot water bottle in my bed will help me sleep.

As well as my own bed here are some other things I'll need –

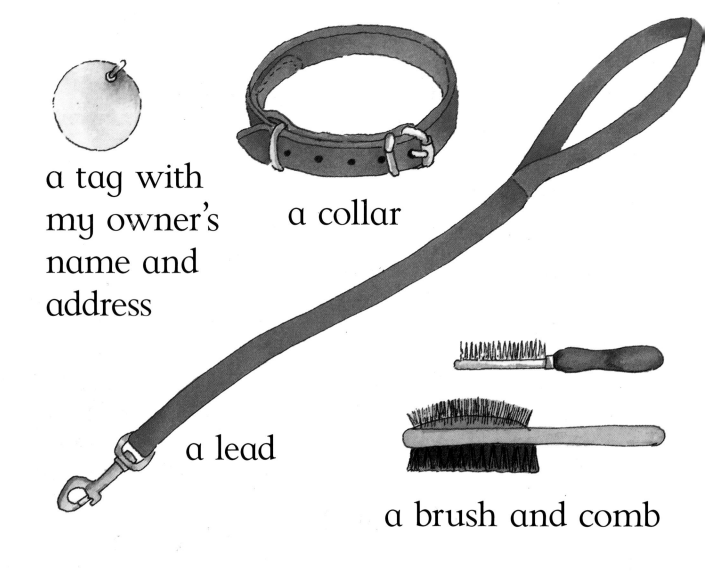

a tag with my owner's name and address

a collar

a lead

a brush and comb

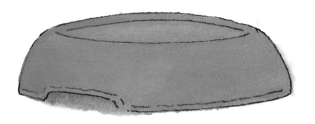

a food bowl

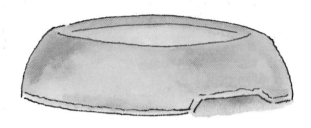

a water bowl

a fork

a spoon

an old towel

and lots of . . .

toys!

I love playing games like chase and tug-of-war. I also like chewing as it makes my teeth strong.

Special tinned puppy food is best for me to eat. Mix it with some dog biscuits so my teeth can crunch them.

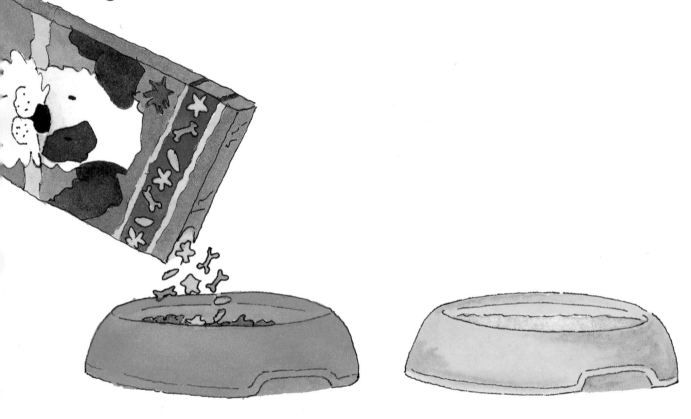

I like drinking water best — milk might make me sick.

Because I'm so little I'll need three or four small meals a day. When I'm grown up two meals a day will be enough.

At first, you'll have to find me a special place for my toilet. Newspapers spread out in a corner will be fine.

I'll always try to get there in time.
But don't be too cross if I miss.

I can play in your garden. When I'm a bit bigger I'll need a walk every day. We could go to the park.

Remember I must have special injections before I can go outside your home. They stop me getting nasty germs from other dogs.

Even though I can't talk, I can make you understand me.

When I do this I want to play.

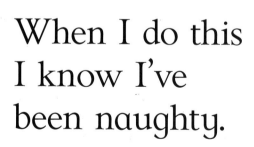

When I do this
I know I've
been naughty.

When I do this I'm cross and growl. It's best to leave me alone.

This is begging — please give me some.

When I'm happy I wriggle and wag my tail. I'm so pleased you've chosen me to be your friend.

A few words for parents

Taking a new puppy into your home is a very important step both for your family and for the puppy. This book will help you to tell your children how they can help the puppy settle into its new family. This may also be a first puppy for you. Don't forget you are taking on responsibility for this new member of your family.

It is a good idea to register with a local veterinary practice as soon as you get your puppy. You will find names and addresses of practices in your local directory. You should ask them about any necessary injections and for advice on worming and feeding. It might be wise to think about pet health insurance in case your puppy needs extensive treatment.

It is a legal requirement that a dog must always carry a tag with the name and address of its owner. It is a good idea to include your telephone number as well. If you are keen to take precautions against theft ask your veterinary practice about identification by means of a tiny microchip which is put just under the skin. This gives lifelong identification and cannot go missing.

Do remember that, just like a human baby, a puppy will require lots of sleep. Don't let your children play too much with it. Puppies love chewing, but make sure they don't chew anything which they could bite off and swallow. As the puppy gets older, it is a good idea to take it to dog training classes.

One last word. Do train your children always to wash their hands after playing with the puppy and especially before they eat any food.

Enjoy your puppy.

Terence Bate BVSc, LLB, MRCVS

Sharing books with your child

Early Worms are a range of books for you to share with your child. Together you can look at the pictures and talk about the subject or story. Listening, looking and talking are the first vital stages in children's reading development, and lay the early foundation for good reading habits.

Talking about the pictures is the first step in involving children in the pages of a book, especially if the subject or story can be related to their own familiar world. When children can relate the matter in the book to their own experience, this can be used as a starting point for introducing new knowledge, whether it is counting, getting to know colours or finding out how other people live.

Gradually children will develop their listening and concentration skills as well as a sense of what a book is. Soon they will learn how a book works: that you turn the pages from right to left, and read the story from left to right on a double page. They start to realize that the black marks on the page have a meaning and that they relate to the pictures. Once children have grasped these basic essentials they will develop strategies for "decoding" the text such as matching words and pictures, and recognising the rhythm of the language in order to predict what comes next. Soon they will start to take on the role of an independent reader, handling and looking at books even if they can't yet read the words.

Most important of all, children should realize that books are a source of pleasure. This stems from your reading sessions which are times of mutual enjoyment and shared experience. It is then that children find the key to becoming real readers.

First published in 1998
This edition published 1999
by Franklin Watts
96 Leonard Street,
London EC2A 4XD

Franklin Watts Australia
14 Mars Road
Lane Cove
NSW 2066

Text and illustrations copyright
© Jakki Wood 1998

Series editor: Paula Borton
Art director: Robert Walster
Photography Steve Shott
With thanks to Ben Ridley-
Johnson.

A CIP catalogue record for this
book is available from the British
Library.

ISBN 0 7496 2837 5 (hbk)
ISBN 0 7496 3500 2 (pbk)

Dewey Classification 636.6

Printed in Belgium

Consultant advice: Sue Robson and Alison Kelly, Senior Lecturers in Education,
Faculty of Education, Early Childhood Centre, Roehampton Institute, London.
Veterinary Advice: Terence Bate BVSc, LLB, MRCVS